Ribbon Embroidery

Heather Joynes

Kangaroo Press

Contents

Conversion table from metric to inches for use in this book:

10 mm = 1 cm
1 cm = ⅜ inch
5 cm = 2 inches
0.5 m = 50 cm = 19¾ inches
1 metre = 39⅜ inches

Where the requirements state 1 metre, 1 yard should be sufficient.
When buying ribbons, 2 metres is a useful quantity.

Cover: Flower Picture

© Heather Joynes

Reprinted 1988, 1989, 1990, 1991, 1992 and 1993

First published in 1988 by Kangaroo Press Pty Ltd
3 Whitehall Road (P.O. Box 75) Kenthurst NSW 2156
Typeset by G.T. Setters Pty Limited
Printed in Hong Kong by Colorcraft Ltd

ISBN 0 86417 184 6

ntroduction

mbroidery with ribbons has been popular since the 3th century, when it was often worked professionlly on court dress for both men and women. Small ems such as workbags, pocketbooks and pinushions were also decorated with ribbon embroiery by amateur needlewomen.

At various periods in the 19th century ribbons ere used to embroider costumes, bags, bookcovers, prons, needlecases, etc. The ribbons used were silk, 1 narrow widths and often shaded. The designs were nvariably floral and worked mostly in arrangements f straight stitches. Chenille and floss silk threads were sometimes combined with the ribbons in simple stitchery.

Today, there is a wonderful range of ribbons with which to work, in velvet, satin, silk, polyester and rayon, and in wide to very narrow widths. Combined with stitchery in the beautiful threads available now, ribbon embroidery becomes a rich and excitingly textured technique which can be applied to all sorts of things including clothing, bags, cushions, boxes, pictures, brooches, and needlecases. Examples of all these articles are illustrated in this book.

Materials

A firm fabric is best for ribbon embroidery. Velvet, elveteen, silk, rayon, linen, cotton and wool are all uitable provided they are firmly woven. Thin fabric s difficult to work on and should be avoided by beginners.

A good range of ribbons is essential. Narrow ibbons in 1.5 mm and 3 mm widths are the most useful. Several shades of a colour give a richer effect han just one shade.

Chenille, tapestry, and crewel needles in several sizes are essential.

A stiletto is useful for piercing holes in the fabric hrough which to pull the ribbon.

Embroidery threads in colours to tone and contrast with your ribbons are recommended. Stranded cotton and Perle Cotton Nos. 5 & 8 are the most useful but any other threads can be used as well. You will also need sewing cotton to match the ribbons.

Both embroidery scissors and a larger pair of scissors are required. An embroidery hoop is sometimes helpful, but care has to be taken to prevent it marking the fabric.

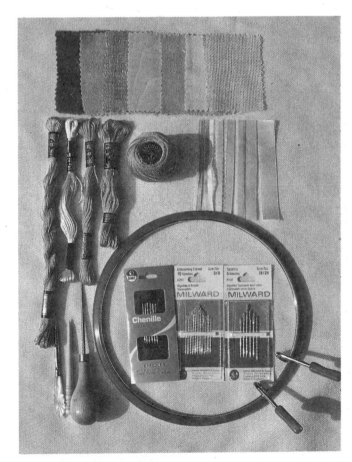

Top row, left to right: Velvet, velveteen, silk, rayon, cotton, wool and linen
Second row, left to right: Perle Cotton 5, rayon thread, Stranded Cotton, Broder Cotton, Perle Cotton 8 and a selection of ribbons
Third row, left to right: Stilettos, antique and new, a spring embroidery hoop, packets of chenille, tapestry and crewel needles.

Starting and Finishing

To start, leave about 1.5 cm of ribbon on the wrong side of the work. This can be sewn down with sewing cotton when part of the work is completed. Finish in the same way. It is essential not to leave long ends behind the work as they would get tangled.

Some polyester ribbons are very springy and need to be sewn down at the back of the work as soon a is practical.

If you have difficulty getting a ribbon through th fabric, use a stiletto to make a hole for the ribbon t pass through.

Stitches

Make stitches large enough for the scale of the ribbon, and work rather more loosely than usual.

If you want the ribbon flat, hold it in place with your thumb while pulling it through the fabric. It can sometimes be effective to let the ribbon twist.

Use stitches that have most of the stitch on the right side of the work—herringbone, chain anc cretan stitches all have a minimum of the stitch or the reverse side.

Threaded stitches can be utilised to make rich patterns. Use a firm thread such as Perle Cotton fo the groundwork stitch.

Fly Stitch   This stitch can be worked singly, in groups with long tails or in horizontal or vertical rows.

4

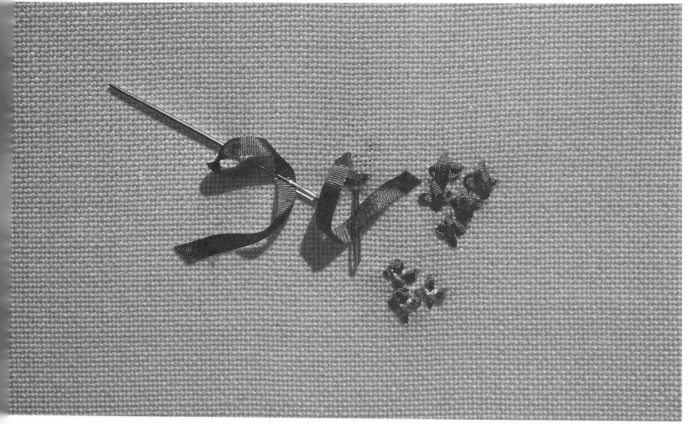

Cross Stitch This stitch can be worked as a vertical or diagonal cross. A cross in the opposite direction can also be worked over the initial cross stitch.

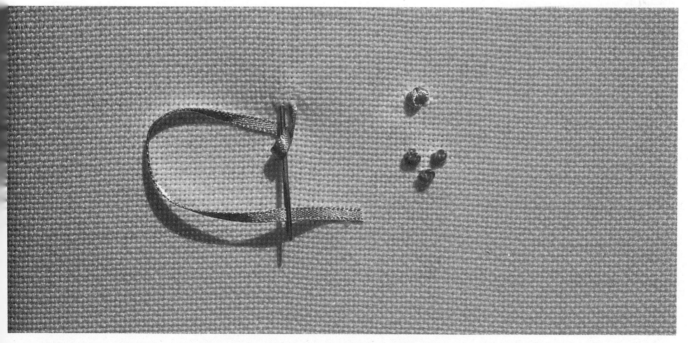

French Knot 1. Bring the thread or ribbon through the fabric, twist it once only around the needle, then insert the needle into the fabric close to the starting point and pull through to the back.

2. Hold the thread firmly with the left thumb while pulling the thread through. When working with satin ribbon leave the knot looser than normal while pulling the ribbon through to the back.

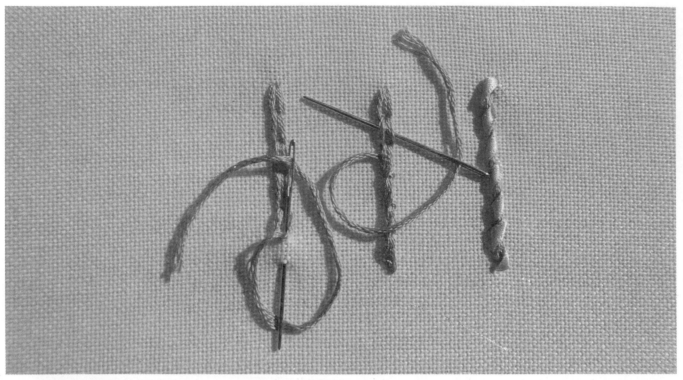

Whipped Chain Stitch Work a row of continuous chain stitch then whip over each stitch with either the same thread or a contrasting colour.

Twisted Chain Stitch The needle goes into the fabric over the thread before making the chain. In ribbon, this stitch makes a good bud.

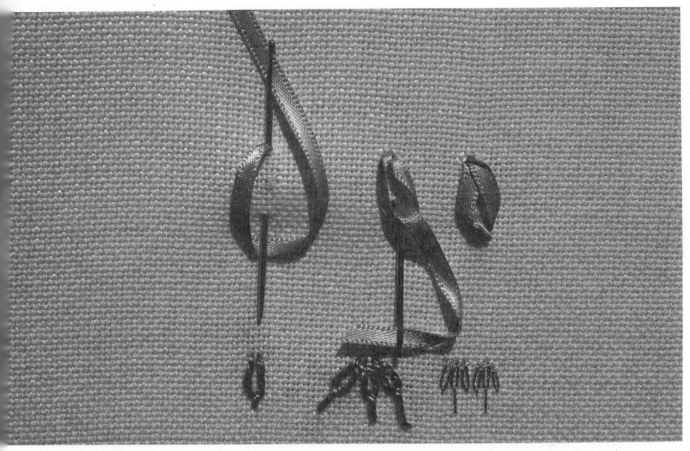

Detached Chain Stitch This stitch can be worked with a short or long stitch at the end.

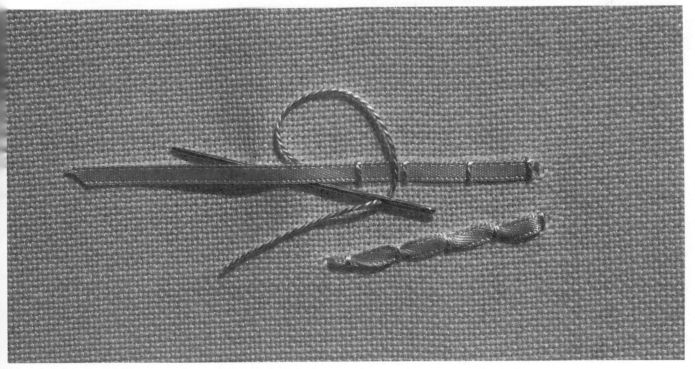

Couching Lay a thread or ribbon along the line to be covered, and with another thread, tie it down with a small stitch at intervals.

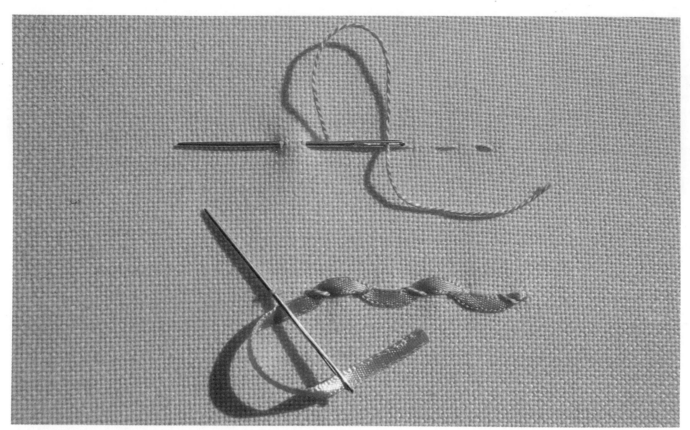

Threaded Running Stitch Work a row of running stitch, then thread in and out of the running stitch with a ribbon or thread.

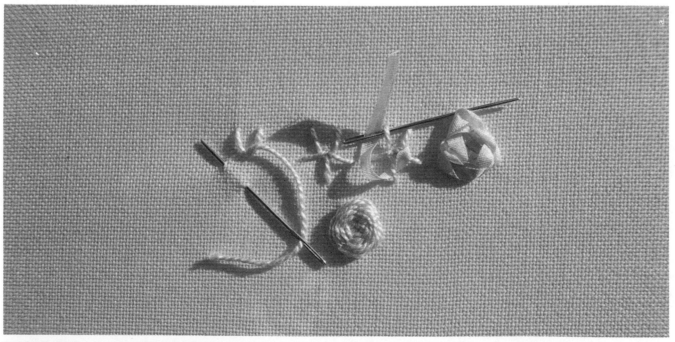

Spider's Web   1. In a firm thread, such as Perle Cotton, work a fly stitch.

2. Add a straight stitch each side of the fly stitch, into the central point.

3. Bring a thread or ribbon through at the centre and weave it over and under the spokes until the web is filled. When using ribbon, weave it fairly loosely and let it twist occasionally, the result is a rose-like circle.

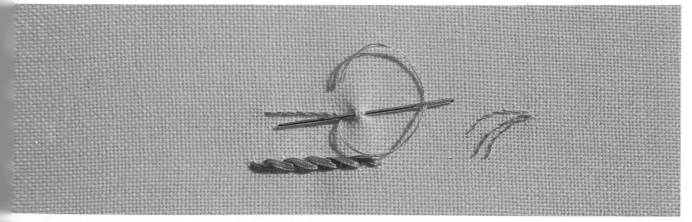

Stem Stitch: This can be worked as a fine line or in close rows to form a filling.

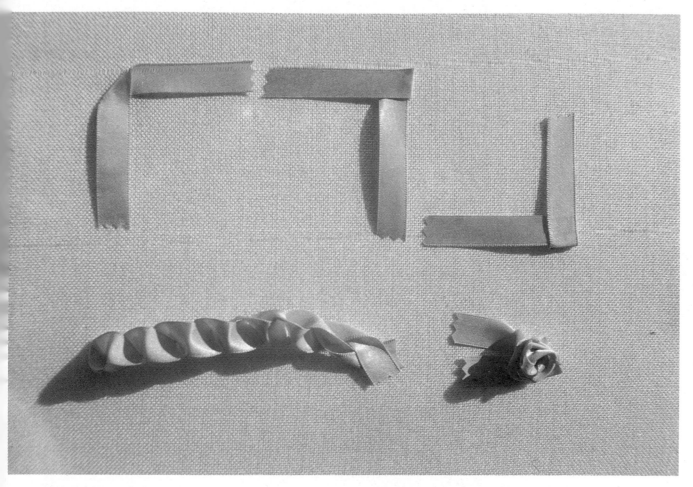

Folded Rose Instructions   Have a needle threaded with matching cotton ready.

1. Fold ribbon as illustrated top left.
2. Fold right side over the left (top centre).
3. Fold lower end up (top right).
4. Repeat 2 and 3 until there are 20 folds.
5. Hold ends in one hand and release folds (bottom left).
6. Hold ends firmly in one hand and then pull one end with the other hand, slowly, until the rose forms (bottom right).
7. Stitch the rose through the centre and once or twice around the petals, as invisibly as possible. This will secure it.
Cut the ends, fold back neatly and sew on to the fabric.

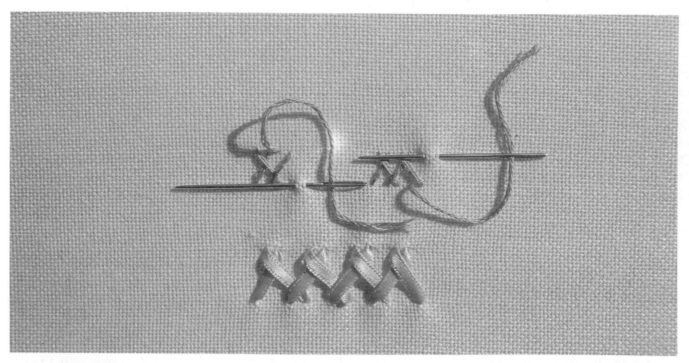

Herringbone Stitch: This stitch can be worked very close or well spaced. It is an ideal stitch to work over ribbon to give a curved line.

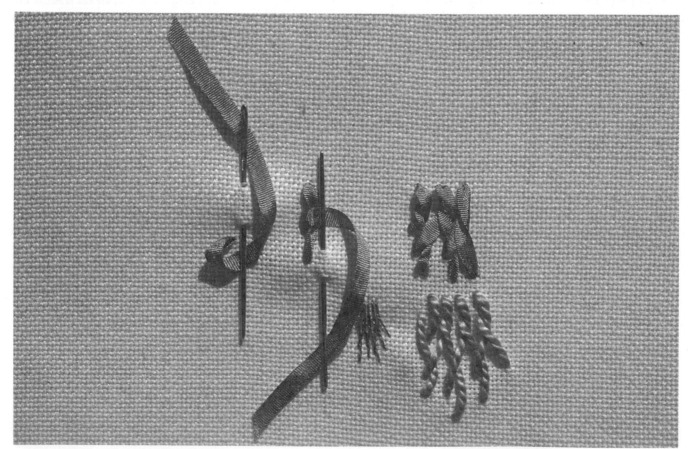

Cretan Stitch   Note that the needle always points inwards, with the thread under it. Cretan stitch is very versatile as it can be worked closely or spaced evenly or unevenly, so that many different textures can be created with it.

Designs

The design must be suitable and in scale for the article you are making. Always work out the size and shape of the item first, then the area to be embroidered, then the details of the design. Details of the design need only be simple, e.g. circles and ovals for flowers and leaves.

Designing for clothing needs special attention as the whole garment has to be considered as well as the person who will wear it.

Cut an extra pattern in paper and mark the area to be embroidered on it, then try it against the person who will wear it. Any adjustments can be made before working up the design of the embroidery. If it is an important garment, it is worth making a calico replica with the design marked on it.

Time spent on planning and designing is time well spent and will save hours of anguished unpicking!

When working on anything with seams that will be under the embroidery, work on each piece of the article to within about 3 cm of the seam, then sew up the seam, press on the wrong side and complete the embroidery over the seam.

Transferring Designs

Ribbon embroidery only needs very simple outlines of the design transferred to the fabric to be embroidered.

For small pieces like brooches or needlecases you only need to mark where the largest elements of the design are (a dot is enough) in pencil or a water-soluble fabric marking pen. The rest of the design can usually be followed from the drawing. For larger more specific designs outline the design on paper with a black felt pen so that it is very clear. Tape this to a flat surface with adhesive tape. Lay a piece of nylon net over the design and attach it with adhesive tape. Go over the outline of the design with a black felt pen, then remove the net and place in position on the fabric to be embroidered. Pin or tack securely in place. Now go over the outline on the net with a water-soluble fabric marking pen. When you remove the net, the outline of the design will appear on your fabric as a series of dots. These dots can be removed when the embroidery is finished by holding a cotton bud damped with water against them.

Finishing

Your finished ribbon embroidery can be pressed lightly on the wrong side into a well-padded surface –a folded towel is ideal. Take care not to flatten the embroidery.

When mounting pictures, make sure the mount is perfectly squared at the corners. If possible use acid-free board.

When using glue, work on clean scrap paper and change the paper after every stage of the construction.

A large darning needle is ideal for spreading glue and for applying a small spot of glue to a small area.

The pieces in this book are a guide and need not be followed slavishly. Do use your own ideas. Change the colours or the stitches. Perhaps you would prefer the design for a bag on a dress, or the picture design on a cushion. Adapt designs to suit yourself, adding your own ideas as they occur to you. The creation of something that is entirely your own work is a most satisfying and joyful experience.

Brooches

These can be initials, circles or any other simple geometric shape. The rich effect is obtained by using several tones of the same colour with a small amount of contrast, and by working the embroidery very densely.

First, on paper, draw the shape you have chosen exactly the size you require, then fill this shape with an arrangement of circles or ovals in different sizes (see Diagram 1—this drawing is the design to work from).

For a design similar to the H brooch you will need:

a piece of fabric about 6 cm square, velveteen, satin, silk or heavy rayon are all suitable.

0.5 m each of 2 tones of 3 mm wide silk or soft polyester ribbon

0.5 m each of 2 tones of 3 mm double-sided satin ribbon

Perle Cotton No. 5 in 2 tones similar to these ribbons

Sewing Cotton in a tone of these colours

0.5 m of 3 mm wide double-sided satin ribbon in a contrast colour

a 6 cm square of firm card or plastic

a 6 cm square of felt or leather for backing

a brooch fastener, which can be brought from a lapidary supply shop.

H Brooch

Key

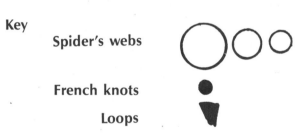

Spider's webs

French knots

Loops

Method:

1. Mark the exact shape of the brooch on the fabric using either a sharp pencil or a water-soluble fabric marking pen.

2. Mark dots for the centres of the larger circles.

3. Work spider's webs over the dots using a variety of the 4 tones of 3 mm ribbons.

4. Add smaller spider's webs in Perle Cotton, then French knots in both ribbon and Perle Cotton to fill the spaces between the spider's webs.

5. Work small loops in the contrasting coloured ribbon last. These need to be well secured at the back of the work with Sewing Cotton.

To make up:

1. Press the embroidery on the wrong side, on a well-padded surface. Cut the card or plastic to the shape required with a craft knife. Lightly sandpaper the edges to smooth them.

2. Cut a piece of felt or leather exactly the same size

as the card. Cut the embroidered fabric 1.5 cm larger all round than the card shape. Carefully clip into corners and curves, allowing enough fabric to cover the card.

3. Spread a little glue onto the back of the card, then wrap the embroidery over the card and adhere to the back. Fold the corners over as neatly as possible. Use a darning needle to add spots of glue where needed.

4. Sew the brooch fastener to the felt or leather backing, which you have already cut out.

5. Glue the backing to the back of the brooch.

For a design similar to the J brooch you will need:

a 6 cm square of fabric

1 m each of 3 mm wide silk or soft polyester ribbon in 3 tones of the same colour

1 m of double-sided satin ribbon in a bright colour

Perle Cotton No. 5 in a tone of the same colour as the satin ribbon, and in a contrasting colour

a 6 cm square of card or plastic

a 6 cm square of felt or leather for backing

a brooch fastener

J Brooch

Method:

1. Mark the shape of the brooch on the fabric with either a sharp pencil or a water-soluble fabric marking pen.

2. Mark dots on the fabric where groups of large French knots will be. Work chain stitches in semi-circles around these dots in the 3 tones of 3 mm wide ribbon.

3. Add French knots in the satin ribbon and one tone of the Perle Cotton.

4. Fill any spaces with French knots in Perle Cotton adding the contrasting colour last.

Make up as for the H brooch.

Key

Detached chain

French knots

Needlecase Set

This charming set consists of a needlecase, scissors case and a pinwheel. The set illustrated has been made in a furnishing moire, but linen, heavy silk, rayon or velveteen would all be suitable. The best results will be obtained by using tones of similar colours, with a small amount of a contrasting colour.

Use the design in Diagram 3 or work out a simple design of your own.

You will need:

⅓ m of fabric

a piece of interfacing 26 cm × 13.5 cm

a piece of flannel 26 cm × 13.5 cm

2 m of 3 mm satin ribbon to tone with the fabric

1.5 m of 3 mm satin ribbon in another tone

2 m each of 2 tones of 3 mm silk or soft polyester ribbon

1 m of 5 mm satin ribbon with a picot edge, to tone with the fabric

Stranded Cotton in a tone of the main colour and a contrasting colour

Sewing Cotton to match the fabric

a piece of firm, thin card or plastic 12 cm × 16 cm approx. (*Note:* plastic from an icecream container is ideal)

Method:

1. Cut a piece of the fabric 30 cm × 17 cm. This allows for 1.5 cm turnings all round. On one 17 cm wide end mark a curved line. Use a sharp pencil or water-soluble fabric marking pen, and make dots rather than a continuous line.

2. Then mark the centres of the larger circles of the design on the fabric 2 cm in from the curved line.

3. Work spider's webs over these dots in the silk or polyester ribbon. Start in the centre of the curve and work outwards, graduating the webs to the outer edge.

4. Now work the large French knots and loops in satin ribbon. Make sure you sew the loops securely on the wrong side.

5. The small crosses are worked next, with 4 small stitches into a central point.

6. Work fly stitch in groups of 2 and 3 stitches around the edge of the design, using 2 strands of Stranded Cotton, with French knots in the same thread at the ends of the fly stitches.

7. Small French knots in a contrasting colour, worked in 2 strands of Stranded Cotton complete the embroidery.

To make up:

1. Cut a piece of interfacing 26 cm × 13.5 cm, and cut a curve at one end, the same as the curve on the fabric.

2. Lightly press the embroidery on the wrong side, into a well-padded surface.

3. Fold the embroidery over the interfacing and tack into place, folding the corners neatly. To get a good curved edge, gather the fabric slightly, using a running stitch, until it curves over the interfacing.

4. Press lightly.

5. Cut the flannel to fit the prepared needlecase so that the edge of the flannel is about 0.5 cm within the edge. Tack into place carefully, so that the stitches do not come through to the right side of the work. Pin the picot-edged ribbon over the tacked edge of the flannel and sew down through the picots, again taking care not to stitch through to the right side of the needlecase.

6. Fold the straight edge up for 6 cm and sew up the sides with neat, small stitches in Sewing Cotton to match the fabric. This forms the pocket to hold the scissors case and pinwheel.

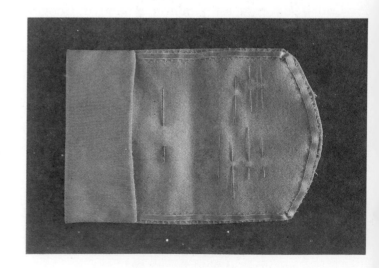

Needlecase

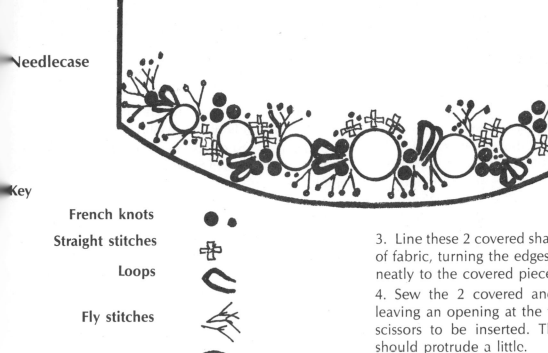

Key

French knots	• •
Straight stitches	+
Loops	⊂
Fly stitches	⋌
Spider's webs	○ ○ ○

The Pinwheel

1. Cut 2 circles of card or plastic 5 cm in diameter.

2. Work a small spray in the same ribbons and threads as for the needlecase on a piece of fabric.

3. Cut the embroidered fabric and one other piece into circles 1.5 cm larger than the card or plastic.

4. Taking care to centre the embroidery, gather the fabric tightly over each circle of card or plastic.

5. Sew the 2 covered circles together with small neat stitches.

6. Couch a 3 mm satin ribbon around the edge, pushing the ends between the 2 sides.

7. Stick pins around the edge. Some Berry Pins as well as ordinary pins look very decorative.

The Scissors Case

1. In card or thin plastic cut 2 shapes, similar to the one illustrated, to fit your scissors.

2. Work a small design in the same ribbons and threads used on the needlecase. Cut out the embroidered fabric and 3 other pieces 1 cm larger than the card or plastic shape. Fold the embroidered fabric and one of the other pieces over the 2 cards or plastic shapes and glue carefully.

3. Line these 2 covered shapes with the other pieces of fabric, turning the edges under and sewing them neatly to the covered pieces.

4. Sew the 2 covered and lined pieces together, leaving an opening at the top large enough for the scissors to be inserted. The bows of the scissors should protrude a little.

5. Couch matching 3 mm ribbon around the edge of the case, starting with the top of the back piece. The ends of the ribbon can be pushed inside the case. Then, starting at the bottom of the case, couch ribbon around the edge, finishing off with a turned-under edge.

Falling Petals Design

This design should fill an area such as a yoke on a jacket or dress, or a shape on a cushion. It could also be adapted to make an all-over pattern for a bag, or for a band of embroidery on clothing, on sleeves for instance.

As the velvet ribbon is pulled through the fabric, a more loosely woven fabric than usual is advisable. The illustration is worked on a wool flannel, but coarse linen or cotton would also be suitable.

The use of a stiletto to make holes for the velvet ribbon to pass through is recommended.

The design looks best in soft tones of 2 close colours, such as the greys and creams in the illustration.

The illustration is of a section 16 cm × 10 cm and the quantities quoted are for this size.

Multiply these quantities for the number of repeats you need.

You will need:

fabric for the item to be made
2 m each of 10 mm and 14 mm velvet ribbon in 2 shades of the same colour
3 m of 3 mm satin ribbon in another colour
Broder Cotton in a tone the same as the velvet ribbon
synthetic raffia in a similar tone
Perle Cotton 5 and a shiny embroidery thread in the colour chosen
Sewing Cotton to match the velvet ribbons

Method:

1. Start with the velvet petals, which are loops of velvet ribbon pulled through the fabric, the ends turned under and stitched down to make a point.

2. Work clusters of French knots in synthetic raffia at the centre of each group of velvet petals.

3. Fly stitch in satin ribbon is worked under the velvet petals, followed by the same stitch in Broder Cotton.

4. Work long detached chains in shiny thread, followed by small French knots in Perle Cotton 5.

Falling Petals

Key

Loops of velvet ribbon

French knots

Fly stitch

Detached chain

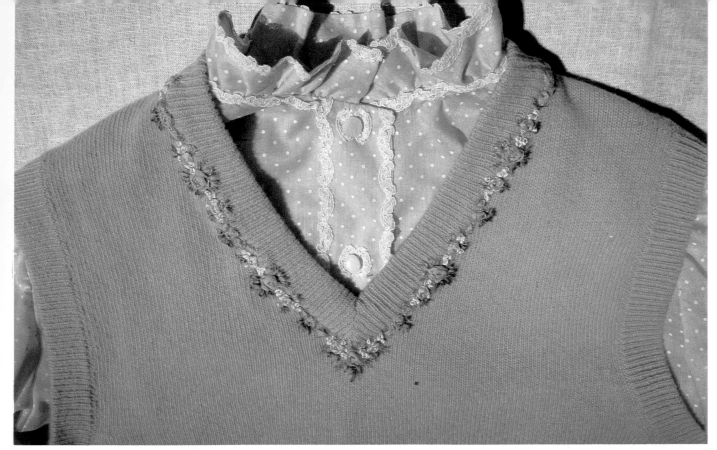

Rose Chain Design (see page 24)

Falling Petals Design (opposite)

17

Knot Flowers (see page 30)

Round Box (see page 22)

Brooches (see page 12)

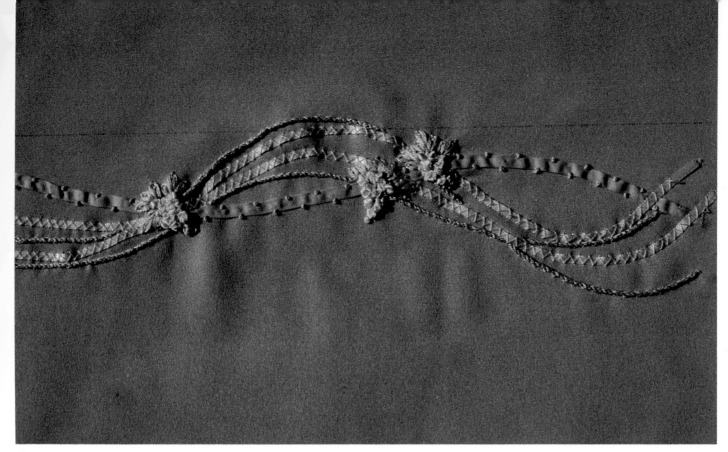

Ribbon Vine Design (see page 31)

Design for a Cushion (see page 26)

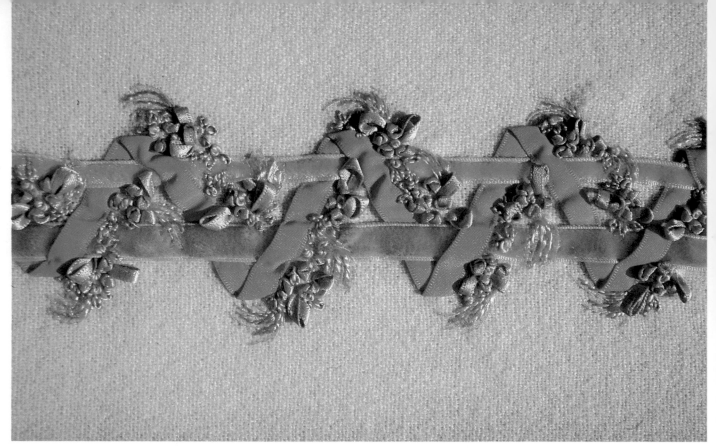

Trellis Design (opposite)

Evening Bag (see page 28)

Trellis Design

This design is suitable as a border for a jacket or yoke, or for a cushion.

The illustration is worked on wool flannel but linen, velvet, velveteen, firm cotton or polyester would be equally suitable.

The quantities quoted are for a design measuring 20 cm long. Multiply these quantities by the number of repeats you require.

The design looks best in a close range of colours.

You will need:

fabric for the item you are making
¼ m each of 10 mm velvet ribbon, 5 mm velvet ribbon and 8 mm soft nylon or polyester ribbon
2 m of 3 mm satin ribbon
2 m of 1.5 mm satin ribbon
Perle Cotton 5
a shiny rayon or silk embroidery thread
Stranded Cotton in the same colour
monofilament nylon thread

Method:

1. First arrange the trellis, laying the 2 velvet ribbons side by side about 1.5 cm apart and pinning them to the fabric.

2. Weave the soft 8 mm ribbon over and under these as in the diagram, and pin.

3. Sew these ribbons down with monofilament nylon thread, so that the stitches show as little as possible.

4. Work groups of French knots in 1.5 mm satin ribbon and Perle Cotton 5, as shown in the diagram.

5. Then work loops of 3 mm satin ribbon.

6. Small detached chain stitches are added next, in shiny thread and then sprays of stem stitch in shiny thread and one strand of Stranded Cotton.

Key

Velvet and nylon ribbons

French knots

Loops

Detached chains

Stem stitch

Trellis Design

Round Box

You will need:

0.5 m of velvet or velveteen
1 m of 8 mm satin ribbon in deep pink
0.5 m of 8 mm satin ribbon in light red
Sewing Cotton in colours to match the ribbons
1 m each of 3 mm satin ribbon in red, orange and deep pink
1 m of 3 mm satin ribbon in pink
2 m silk or soft polyester ribbon in green
Perle Cotton in red and 2 shades of pink
Stranded Cotton in Jacaranda Blue
a 250 g tin, empty and clean, with cut off lid (*Note:* salmon or cat food tins are ideal)
a strip of felt or flannel 28 cm × 4 cm
firm and light-weight cardboard
a small piece of dacron wadding
fabric glue

Round Box

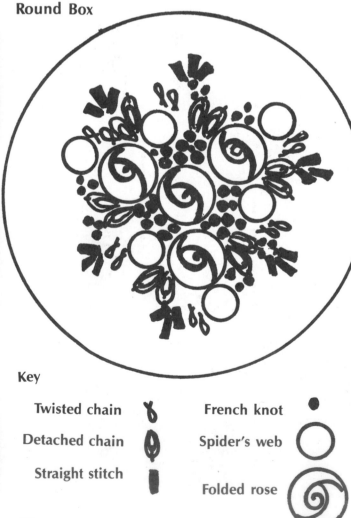

Key

Twisted chain	8	**French knot**	●
Detached chain		**Spider's web**	○
Straight stitch		**Folded rose**	◎

Method:

1. Cut a piece of velvet or velveteen about 16 cm square. Mark the centre with a tacking stitch, and tack a circle around it the size of the design.

2. Make a folded rose in the 8 mm red satin ribbon and 3 of the 8 mm pink satin ribbon.

3. Sew these to the centre of the design as shown in the diagram.

4. Work French knots in red, pink and orange satin ribbon, densely around the roses.

5. Add a few knots in Jacaranda Blue Stranded Cotton, using it double (12 strands).

6. Work spider's webs in red Perle Cotton, then groups of detached chains, working 2 chains one inside the other for each petal.

7. Spider's webs in pink Perle Cotton are worked next, then pairs of twisted chains in 3 mm pink satin ribbon.

8. Add groups of French knots in red and pink Perle Cotton to fill out the circular design, then work groups of 3 straight stitches in green silk or soft polyester ribbon.

To make up the box:

1. Glue a strip of felt or flannel to the side of the tin, between the top and bottom ridges. Leave a gap of about 1.5 cm at the seam of the tin. This is to accommodate the seam in the fabric covering.

2. Measure the circumference of the tin over the felt, and add 3 cm. Measure the depth of the tin, double it and add 4 cm. Cut a piece of velvet or velveteen on the cross or bias to these measurements.

3. Seam the velvet, taking in a little more seam in just under half the seam length. This wider seam will be *inside* the tin.

4. Turn right-side-out, flatten seam and ease over the tin, with the seam over the gap in the felt, and the narrower part of the seam to the outside of the tin. Leave 3 cm of fabric extending at the base of the tin. Run a little fabric glue around the ridge on the base of the tin. Work a running stitch in firm thread around the edge of the fabric at the base of the tin and gather until it fits firmly over the base of the tin. Press the fabric into the glue around the ridge.

Run a little glue around the inside join at the base of the tin, being careful not to get too much glue on the tin.

Put a little glue on the inside seam of the tin. Turn the excess fabric over to the inside of the tin, stretching it slightly and press into the glue at the base of the tin. Work around the inside of the tin a little at a time. It takes practice to get a really neat finish with no wrinkles.

5. Cut a circle of fabric 2 cm wider all round than the tin lid. Gather it over the lid with firm thread, then glue it to the base of the tin and put a weight on it for a while.

6. Cut a circle of light-weight cardboard to fit easily into the covered tin. Lightly glue a circle of dacron wadding to the cardboard then cover with a circle of fabric gathered over it. This should fit into the tin very snugly, and does not really need to be glued in.

7. Cut a circle of cardboard for the lid, 1 cm wider in diameter than the covered tin. Glue a piece of dacron wadding the same size, to the cardboard. Cut the embroidered fabric 2 cm wider all round than the cardboard, taking care to centre the embroidery. Gather over the padded cardboard with a firm thread, and pull tight, so that the fabric is stretched firmly over the lid.

8. Cut a circle of thin cardboard to fit easily into the tin, and cover this with fabric, gathering it over the cardboard. Carefully glue this to the inside of the lid. Always put the glue on the lining, never the lid. Press together firmly, then lay in the top of the tin with the top of the lid to the inside of the tin and put a weight on the lining for a short while.

The lining of the lid should fit snugly into the tin and keep the lid on.

Rose Chain Design

This pretty chain of roses can be embroidered on knitwear, blouses, dresses, or children's wear, and looks well in many different colour combinations.

The illustration is worked on a commercially made knitted wool vest and the quantities quoted are for this garment.

You will need:

6 m of silk or soft polyester 3 mm ribbon in the main colour

4 m of silk or soft polyester 3 mm ribbon in another tone

4 m of 1.5 mm satin ribbon in a contrasting colour

4 m of silk or soft polyester 3 mm ribbon in another colour

Stranded Cotton in the main colour, in another shade of this colour, and in the contrasting colour

Method:

1. Starting with the largest rose, central in the design, work a spider's web in silk or polyester ribbon in the main colour.

2. On each side of the rose work 3 French knots in contrasting satin ribbon.

3. Then, on each side of the knots work a smaller spider's web in the other tone of the main colour in silk or polyester ribbon, followed by 3 more knots in satin ribbon and one underneath the rose, then a twisted chain and a small spider's web in silk or polyester ribbon in the main colour.

4. In a contrasting colour of silk or polyester ribbon work groups of fly stitches under the roses, as in the diagram.

5. Work fly stitches in 2 strands of Stranded Cotton over the ribbon stitches, in a similar colour.

Rose Chain

Key

Spider's webs	
French knots	
Fly stitch	
Detached chain	
Cretan stitch	

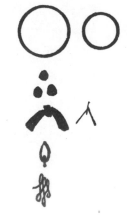

6. Groups of 3 cretan stitches in 2 strands of Stranded Cotton in the main colour are worked each side of the fly stitches under the largest rose, and also above it, and each side of the twisted chain stitch.

7. Small detached chains, in 2 strands of Stranded Cotton in a tone of the main colour are worked above some of the roses (see the diagram).

8. The pattern is then repeated.

Note:

You may have to adjust the pattern to fit the article you are embroidering, as at the point of the V of the vest illustrated. This is not difficult and usually means condensing the pattern slightly. When embroidering a design on something like the vest illustrated, start at the centre front—the V in this case—and work each side alternately to get an even balance.

Design for a Cushion

Lace, ribbons, threaded stitches and roses combine to make a rich texture on this wide band of embroidery. The illustration has been worked on calico but linen, firm cotton or velveteen would also be suitable. The cushion can be finished with a frill of fabric or lace or both, and a zip fastener at the back is recommended.

The cushion illustrated measures 45 cm square, excluding frill.

You will need:

¾ m of fabric 115 cm wide. This includes a frill of single fabric (add another ¼ m if frill is to be double fabric)

1.5 m of 3 cm coarse cotton lace—this is for the cushion only (add 3.5 m for a lace frill)

2 m of 10 mm velvet ribbon

2 m of 5 mm picot-edged satin ribbon — all these ribbons to be in different shades of the same colour

3 m of 3 mm satin ribbon

3 m of 1.5 mm satin ribbon

3 m of 15 mm satin ribbon

6 m of 3 mm cream satin ribbon to match lace

Perle Cotton 8 in cream and main colour

Sewing Cotton in cream and main colour

Method:

1. Cut a piece of fabric 48 cm square. Zig-zag by machine around the edge.

2. Hand sew the lace down the centre and two strips 5.5 cm each side of the central strip.

3. Work spider's webs at regular intervals down the centre of each strip of lace, using cream satin ribbon. Use the pattern of the lace as a guide.

4. Work running stitch in cream Perle Cotton about 0.5 cm from each side of the lace and thread with 3 mm satin ribbon in one of the main shades. Do not pull the ribbon tightly.

5. Next, tack a strip of the picot-edged ribbon beside the threaded running stitch. Attach it to the fabric by working French knots through each picot in Perle Cotton, using cream and the main colour alternately.

6. Now tack a length of 10 mm velvet ribbon down the centre of the space between the picot-edged ribbon.

7. Attach it to the fabric with detached chains in Perle Cotton, about 1.5 cm apart.

8. Then work a row of running stitches using Perle Cotton in the main colour, just inside the detached chains. Thread this with the 1.5 mm satin ribbon.

9. Make 2 sets of double loops in velvet ribbon and sew diagonally across the velvet stripes.

10. Make 6 folded roses from the 15 mm satin ribbon and sew in 2 groups of 3 to the centre of the velvet loops.

To make up the cushion:

1. Cut a piece of fabric 48 cm × 51 cm.

2. Cut this in half across the 51 cm length, and sew a zip fastener to join the 2 halves together, taking in 1.5 cm seams.

3. Round off the corners of the embroidered side of the cushion. Cut, hem and gather the frill and tack around edge.

4. Place the back and front right-sides-together, with the zip opened, and stitch around the edge. Trim the seam and overcast with zig-zag or by hand.

5. Turn right-side-out and press carefully.

Design for a Cushion

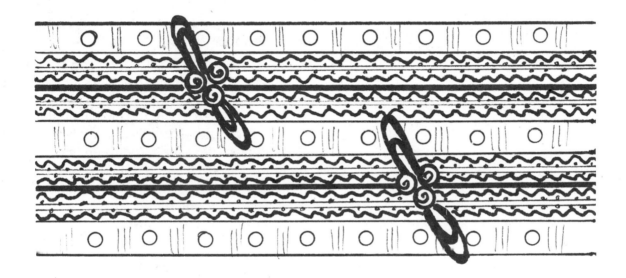

Key	
Lace	
Spider's web	○
Folded rose	◉
Velvet ribbon	
Picot-edged ribbon and French knots	
Threaded running stitch	

27

Evening Bag

This design involves the traditional Indian method of attaching small pieces of mirror, called *shisha* to fabric. These can be bought at some needlework shops. Large sequins can also be used in the same way.

You will need:

a piece of velvet or velveteen 45 cm × 28 cm
a piece of lining fabric 45 cm × 28 cm
a piece of interfacing 45 cm × 28 cm
20 cm of velcro 1.5 cm wide
45 cm of ribbon 7–8 cm wide
7 pieces of *shisha* or sequins
2 m of silver ribbon 3 mm wide
1 m of satin ribbon 1.5 mm wide
Broder Cotton to tone with the ribbon
Stranded Cotton to tone with ribbon and a soft contrasting colour
silver beads
1 m of 3 mm silk ribbon in a soft contrasting colour

Method:

1. Working on the wide ribbon start with the largest circle in the design.

2. Attach the mirror or sequin as shown in the illustration opposite. Work a circle of running stitches around it about 1 cm from the mirror.

3. Bring the silver ribbon through near the mirror and work cretan stitch over the framework attaching the mirror and the running stitch around the mirror. This is instead of pulling the ribbon through the fabric. Take care to keep the ribbon flat while working the stitches. The end of the ribbon can be taken behind the mirror and then cut off.

4. Work groups of cretan stitches, in 2 strands of Stranded Cotton in the contrasting colour, between the ribbon stitches.

5. Sew a bead at the end of each ribbon stitch.

6. Work 2 circles with mirrors and the 1.5 mm ribbon in the same manner, with groups of cretan stitches in 2 strands of Stranded Cotton in a colour of the same tone as the ribbon. Sew a bead at the end of each ribbon stitch.

7. The other 4 circles are worked with mirrors and Broder Cotton to tone with the wide ribbon background. The circle at each end of the design has

Evening Bag

Key

Cretan stitch in ribbon

Cretan stitch in thread

Beads

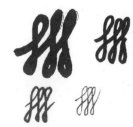

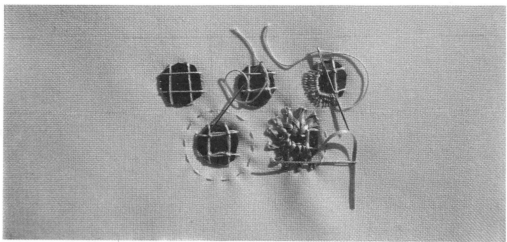

Attaching *shisha* or sequins

cretan stitch worked around it in one strand of Stranded Cotton in the contrasting colour. Sew beads around the 4 circles.

8. Circular groups of beads are sewn at intervals down each side of the design.

9. Centre the embroidered ribbon on the velveteen, tack it carefully in place, then sew each side to the velvet over the contrasting silk ribbon. It is easiest to tuck the silk ribbon under the wide ribbon as you sew it.

10. Sew a length of the silver ribbon at the side of the contrasting ribbon.

To make up:

1. Cut the piece of interlining 1.5 cm smaller all round than the velvet.

2. Fold the velvet over the edge of the interfacing and sew down, taking care not to take the stitches through to the front.

3. Turn under the lining and sew neatly to the prepared velvet. Right sides together, fold up the end not embroidered to the required length for the bag and sew each side firmly together. Turn right-side-out and press very carefully. Sew the velcro fastening to the underside of the flap and to the bag.

Knot Flowers

Here is a way to use those left-over lengths of ribbon. Simply tie them in knots, singly or several together and sew them to fabric. Add some fine ribbon stalks to make an attractive bunch of flowers.

This idea can be used on clothing, bags and small pictures, the knot flowers on their own or with other ribbon flowers.

The illustration is of cards, which are easy and quick to make.

To make a card 10 cm × 14 cm you will need:
a piece of lightweight, coloured cardboard
   30 cm × 14 cm
a small piece of fabric 8 cm × 12 cm
several short lengths of ribbon 4–5 cm long
short lengths of green ribbon
Sewing Cotton
fabric glue

Method:

1. Tie the short lengths of ribbon in knots.

2. Arrange the knot flowers on the fabric and sew down carefully. Sew on the stalks.

3. On the inside of the cardboard, mark 2 lines 10 cm from each end of the 30 cm length. Fold inwards on these lines. Out of the centre panel cut a window 6 cm × 10 cm. This leaves a border of 2 cm all round.

4. With fabric glue, stick the embroidered fabric over the window. Always put the glue on the card, and not too near the edge.

5. Trim a fraction off the end of the card at the left of the back of the embroidery.

6. Lightly glue this side around the edge **only**, and press over the back of the embroidery.

7. Fold firmly down the other fold. It helps to place cards under a book for a short while, to flatten them.

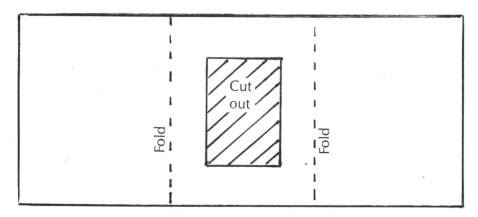

Ribbon Vine Design

This design is suitable for blouses or lingerie. The section illustrated can be repeated and used horizontally or vertically.

The illustration is worked on synthetic georgette, but silk or any other fine fabric would be equally suitable. Read the introductory section on design, with regard to clothing.

You will need:

enough fabric for the garment

Note: the following amounts of ribbon are quoted for one design only—multiply by however many repeats you need:

0.5 m of 5 mm soft polyester ribbon to tone with fabric

1 m of 3 mm satin ribbon

Perle Cotton 8 to match the ribbons

Stranded Cotton to match the ribbons

1 m each of 3 mm satin ribbon in 2 colours contrasting with the fabric

Perle Cotton 8 in one of these colours

Method:

1. Transfer the design to the fabric as described on page 11.

2. Tack the 5 mm ribbon to the appropriate line of the design, being very careful to get a smoothly curved line.

3. Attach the ribbon to the fabric with French knots using 4 strands of Stranded Cotton.

4. Tack 2 lines of satin ribbon and attach them with herringbone stitch over the ribbon, using one strand of Stranded Cotton.

5. Work whipped chain over the other 2 lines.

6. Work French knots in 2 colours of 3 mm satin ribbon in groups. Use more of one colour than the other. Work French knots in Perle Cotton 8 to make a dense bunch with the satin ribbon knots.

7. Using 3 strands of Stranded Cotton, work groups of double chains, one inside the other, at the top of the clusters of knots.

Ribbon Vine Design

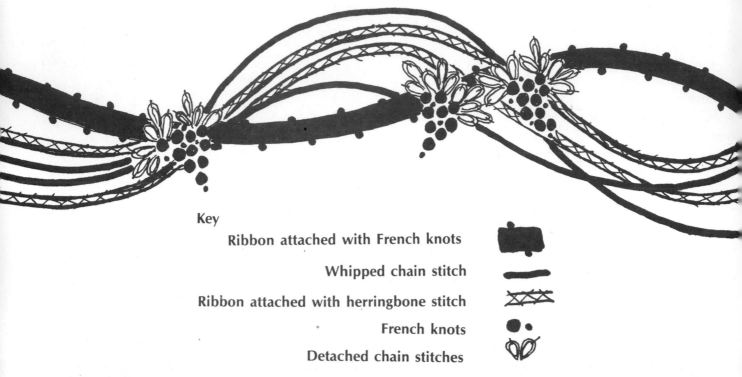

Key

Ribbon attached with French knots	
Whipped chain stitch	
Ribbon attached with herringbone stitch	
French knots	
Detached chain stitches	

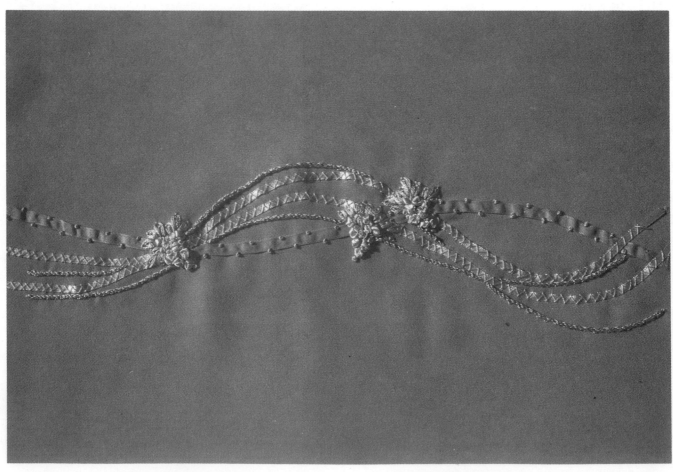

Flower Picture

The types of flowers that can be worked in ribbon vary enormously. You may like to design your own picture, using some of the ideas for flowers in this book.

For a picture similar to the one illustrated, you will need:

a piece of fabric about 30 cm × 25 cm in a neutral colour—velveteen, firm silk, rayon and linen or linen and polyester are all suitable (the picture illustrated is worked on linen and polyester)

1 m of 1 cm wide velvet ribbon

0.5 m of 3 mm satin ribbon to tone with the velvet ribbon

2 m of shaded knitting ribbon, or 3 mm wide soft ribbon in 2 shades.

1.5 m of 5 mm single-sided satin ribbon

2 m each of 2 shades of 3 mm silk or soft polyester ribbon

2 m of 3 mm silk or soft polyester ribbon in a contrasting colour

Perle Cotton in 2 shades of green and a shade to tone with the contrasting coloured ribbon

Stranded Cotton in 3 shades of green and 2 shades of the colour chosen for the 3 sprays at the top of the design

Method:

1. Work the largest flowers first. In the design illustrated these are the velvet ribbon flowers, worked in straight stitches, the stitches being left fairly loose. Work a French knot in the centre of each flower in 3 mm satin ribbon.

2. Next, work detached chain stitches between the velvet petals, using silk or soft polyester ribbon.

3. The groups of roses are worked in shaded knitting ribbon or soft ribbon in 2 shades.

4. Then work a cluster of French knots in the single-sided satin ribbon.

5. Groups of small flowers in a contrasting colour are worked next, using silk or soft polyester ribbon in a straight cross stitch.

6. Another cross stitch in Perle Cotton is worked over the ribbon stitch.

7. The 2 sprays in knitting ribbon or soft ribbon are worked with twisted chain stitch.

8. The 3 sprays at the top of the design are worked in detached chain stitches, starting with narrow stitches in 2 strands of Stranded Cotton, then adding detached chain stitches in silk or polyester ribbon.

9. Three groups of 3 detached chains are next, using silk or soft ribbon in the same colour as the stitches between the velvet petals.

10. The leaves are detached chains, worked one inside the other and in groups. Use Perle Cotton.

11. Other leaves are worked in fly stitch, making stitches one underneath the other in groups of 3 or 4, again in Perle Cotton.

12. The soft background around the flower posy is worked with fly stitches with long tails, in one strand of Stranded Cotton. Work in 3 shades, using the darkest colour at the base of the design, and the lightest around the top.

13. French knots in silk or soft polyester ribbon are scattered among the fly stitches.

14. The picture can be framed as it is or a fabric-covered mount added before framing.

Flower Picture

Key

 Spider's webs   Twisted chains

 French knots

 Detached chains   Straight stitch

 Fly stitch   Cross stitch

34

To frame the picture you will need:

a piece of cardboard, preferably acid-free, the size to fit the frame
fabric glue

Method:

1. Centre the embroidery on the cardboard, making sure the weave of the fabric is straight. Place face down on a clean soft surface, such as a towel.

2. Cut a small amount of fabric from each corner, leaving enough to fold over the corners to the back of the card (see Diagram).

3. Using fabric glue stick down first the corners, then the top and bottom, then the sides. The corners should be mitred, as shown in the diagrams, and sometimes need to be sewn to get a really neat finish.

To make a fabric-covered mount you will need:

a piece of fabric 5 cm larger all round than the mounted picture
a piece of card the same size as the picture
fabric glue

Method:

1. Cut the centre out of the card to the shape desired. Pre-cut mounts can be bought from framing suppliers, and these save a lot of time and trouble.

2. Cover the mount in the same way as for the picture. Then cut the centre from the mount, leaving a 2 cm turning.

3. Clip carefully into corners or around curves.

4. Spread a small amount of glue onto the back of the mount, around the central hole.

5. Carefully fold the fabric over the edge of the centre of the mount, and adhere this to the back of the mount.

6. The mount can then be glued over the picture, taking care not to have any glue too near the centre edge. Accidental glue spots can sometimes be removed by lifting off the glue with a needle. This needs to be done before the glue sets.

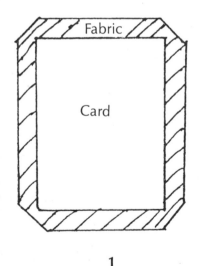

1

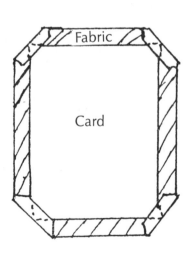

2

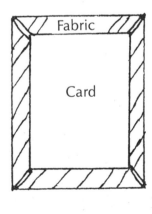

3

Framing the Flower Picture

Individual Flowers

Daisy: 3 mm silk or polyester ribbon, green and yellow Perle Cotton 8.

Two straight stitches are used for each petal. Work the leaves in fly stitch. Work the flower centres with a French knot.

Heath: 3 mm pink satin ribbon, 3 mm green silk ribbon, green Stranded Cotton, white Perle Cotton 8.

Work the flowers in straight stitches in pink satin ribbon, with a fly stitch with a long tail over the straight stitch using white Perle Cotton. Work the leaves in fly stitch in silk ribbon and Stranded Cotton.

Forget-me-not: 3 mm blue silk or polyester ribbon, yellow Perle Cotton 8, green Stranded Cotton.

Work the flowers in 5 small straight stitches with a French knot in the centre in Perle Cotton. Work the stalks in fly stitch and the leaves in detached chain stitch using 4 strands of Stranded Cotton.

Fuchsia: 5 mm magenta satin ribbon, 3 mm purple silk or polyester ribbon, 3 mm green silk or polyester ribbon, Sewing Cotton to match purple ribbon, green Stranded Cotton.

The flower is 3 loops of purple ribbon sewn down at the tips. Add 4 straight stitches, twisted, in magenta satin ribbon. The half-open flower is all straight stitches, as are the bud and leaves. The stems are worked in stem stitch.

Violet: 3 mm silk or polyester ribbon, green Stranded Cotton.

The flowers are worked in straight stitches, 2 to each petal. The leaves are in stem stitch.

Wattle: 3 mm yellow silk or polyester ribbon in yellow and green, yellow Perle Cotton 8, green Stranded Cotton.

Work leaves first in straight stitches in ribbon, 2 stitches to each leaf. Work flowers in silk ribbon in French knots with knots in Perle Cotton at the tips of the sprays. The stem is in stem stitch using Stranded Cotton.

Waratah: 3 mm silk or polyester ribbon in 2 shades of red, 5 mm dark red satin ribbon, red Perle Cotton 5, green Stranded Cotton.

Work straight stitches in 2 shades of red ribbon, the French knots at the top of the flower in Perle Cotton. The sepals are worked in straight stitches, twisted, in satin ribbon. Work the leaves in fly stitch using 3 strands of Stranded Cotton.

Flannel Flower: white 3 mm silk or polyester ribbon, green Stranded Cotton.

Work the flowers in detached twisted chains. Satin-stitch the centre in Stranded Cotton. Work the leaves in fly stitch using 4 strands of Stranded Cotton.

Wisteria: 3 mm mauve silk or polyester ribbon, green Stranded Cotton.

Work the flowers in detached chains with small straight stitches at the tips of the sprays. Work the stalks in stem stitch in 3 strands of Stranded Cotton.

Pinks: 5 mm pink satin ribbon, 3 mm green silk ribbon, pink Sewing Cotton.

Gather one edge of the pink satin ribbon and sew it into a circle for the full flowers. Make profile flowers out of 2 lengths of gathered ribbon, sewn down one under the other. Work the stems in stem stitch and leaves in straight stitches, both in green silk ribbon.

Individual Flowers (opposite)